BETTER BUSINESS COMMUNICATION

I0486397

A *QUICK* GUIDE TO

BETTER WRITING
&
GRAMMAR

HEATHER WRIGHT

Heather Wright
hwrightwriter@gmail.com

Book Layout ©2013 BookDesignTemplates.com

Better Business Communication
A Quick Guide to Better Writing and Grammar/ Heather Wright. —1st ed.

ISBN 978-1517556747
Saugeen Publishers

Get the entire Better Business Communication series in **ONE, COST-SAVING VOLUME**!

The complete contents of

A Quick Guide to Writing Better Email

A Quick Guide to Better Writing & Grammar

A Quick Guide to Better Presentations, and

A Quick Guide to Better Telephone Skills are all **here**:

Better Business Communication

A *QUICK* GUIDE TO

**BETTER EMAIL,
PRESENTATIONS,
TELEPHONE SKILLS,
WRITING &
GRAMMAR**

Heather Wright

Check your online bookstore for more details

Contents

Introduction

This book is **your quick guide to better writing and grammar**. The tips in this book will help you develop the strategies you need to find and correct errors that can reflect badly on you as a professional. This book doesn't cover every grammar, punctuation, and writing problem, but it is designed to hit the most common errors that might be holding you back from producing clean, correct writing.

Bad grammar can cost you money. If that alone isn't a motivator, consider this. How can clients trust you with a detailed financial project you are doing on their behalf, when you can't be bothered to pay attention to the details of spelling and grammar?

Or consider this: you are just starting in the workplace and the people you work for or want to work for aren't your generation. They don't communicate in the same way that your friends do via text and in person. If you want to impress employers, get the grammar right.

Employers consider good writing and speaking skills as the *minimum* skills you should have in order to be a competent worker. If your work doesn't meet those standards, then how can you represent their company at a higher level? Their employees are their companies' ambassadors; they want their ambassadors to impress not embarrass.

Yes, checking your work for grammar and spelling errors will take a little extra time, but consider it an investment in your career. As you learn to recognize and correct your errors, you should eventually stop making them in the first place, and you'll get back up to speed again.

Here are four articles that might convince you that spelling and grammar matter:

1. "Spelling and Grammar Matter in Marketing" by Kara Sassone. Kara links to other articles that demonstrate the benefits of good grammar and spelling.
http://blog.hubspot.com/blog/tabid/6307/bid/20383/Why-Spelling-and-Grammar-Matter-in-Marketing.aspx

2. CEO Kyle Weins explains in the *Harvard Business Review* why he won't hire people with poor grammar skills.
https://hbr.org/2012/07/i-wont-hire-people-who-use-poo

3. "Realtor listings: Bad grammar and typos cost agents money, according to U.S. study" by Shari Kulha.
http://news.nationalpost.com/homes/realtor-listings-bad-grammar-and-typos-cost-agents-money-according-to-u-s-study

4. "Bad Grammar Will Lose Your Online Business Money" by Jason Walker.
http://www.searchandmore.co.uk/internet-marketing/bad-grammar-lose-online-business-money/

Other books previously released in this Better Business Communication series cover presentations, emails, telephone skills, and improving your writing and grammar. All are available at your online bookseller.

Better Business Communication
A **QUICK** GUIDE TO
BETTER TELEPHONE SKILLS

Heather Wright

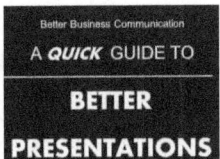

Better Business Communication
A **QUICK** GUIDE TO
BETTER PRESENTATIONS

Heather Wright

Better Business Communication
A **QUICK** GUIDE TO
WRITING BETTER EMAILS

Heather Wright

Better Business Communication
A **QUICK** GUIDE TO
BETTER EMAIL, PRESENTATIONS, TELEPHONE SKILLS, WRITING & GRAMMAR

Heather Wright

CHAPTER 1

Tip 1: Avoid Wordiness

No this isn't a grammar or a spelling error, but wordiness will hurt the first impression that your writing makes with your readers. I know that you want to sound courteous and respectful to your reader, but that can translate into wasting the reader's time with a lot of unnecessary words. You may be very polite, but none of that matters if your reader is inwardly screaming, "Get to the point!" You also need to respect your reader's time. Don't waste it; instead, choose the following options.

One word instead of many

It's easy to get carried away with your own words, especially when you are trying to make an impression. Simpler is better and you can still be polite without being wordy. The following is an example of a wordy email message:

Thank you so much for kindly responding to my inquiry so quickly. The committee and I were very pleased to read your response and are very honoured that you have agreed to speak to our managers on the 14th. In response to your request for suggested topics for your speech, we have surveyed our manag-

ers who were very happy to reply to our request. Here are the topics that they have suggested. (72 words)

Instead, consider this:

Thanks for getting back to me so quickly. We really appreciate your agreeing to speak to our managers on the 14th. You asked for some possible topics, and my managers suggested the following: (33 words)

Sometimes we get into bad habits and uses stock phrases without realizing that there are less wordy alternatives. Here are some examples of groups of words that can be replaced by just one.

Some groups of words say the same things twice:

Mutual agreement	An agreement, by definition, has to be mutual.
Future prospects	Prospects are always in the future
Advance warning	If a warning isn't in advance, it's not much use.

You get the idea. There are lots of other groups of words that can be replaced by a simpler option.

At this point in time	Now, Today
Make an assumption	Assume
In today's society	Today
Came to a realization	Realized

Here is a link to a comprehensive list of words you can eliminate or change to avoid wordiness in your writing:
http://web.uvic.ca/~gkblank/wordiness.html

Organize

Put your ideas into short paragraphs. When you change topic, make a new paragraph. Nothing looks less appealing to read than one long dense piece of text on a page.

Thanks for getting back to me so quickly. We really appreciate your agreeing to speak to our managers on the 14th. You asked for some possible topics. Here are some that my managers suggested. They wanted you to talk about the latest changes to Product C. They also wanted information about introducing customers to our new website. Could you also tell them about the expansion to the eastern headquarters? Many managers wanted to know if you spotted any new trends at the Waterloo convention you attended. I'll be sending you the full program for the meeting as soon as it is complete. If you have any questions, please contact me at ext. 234.

Thanks again.

Here's how the message looks now with paragraphs and a bullet list to help organize the information in a way that is accessible by the reader:

Thanks for getting back to me so quickly. We really appreciate your agreeing to speak to our managers on the 14th.

You asked for some possible topics. Here are some that my managers suggested:

1) The latest changes to product C
2) Strategies for introducing customers to the new website
3) An update on the expansion of the eastern headquarters

4) Any new trends that you spotted at the Waterloo convention

I'll be sending you the full program for the meeting as soon as it is complete. If you have any questions, please contact me at ext. 234.

Thanks again.

Heather

IN SHORT

- Use one word instead of many.
- Organize ideas into short paragraphs
- Use bullet point lists

CHAPTER 2

Tip 2: Use Bullet Point Lists to Organize Data

Lists hidden in paragraphs look like long unbroken clumps of words on the screen and are not reader-friendly. Here's an example of a wordy paragraph from the previous chapter:

You asked for some possible topics. Here are some that my managers suggested. They wanted you to talk about the latest changes to Product C. They also wanted information about introducing customers to our new website. Could you also tell them about the expansion to the eastern headquarters? Many managers wanted to know if you spotted any new trends at the Waterloo convention you attended.

The above paragraph is wordy and the ideas in it can be explained more clearly using bullet points, as below:

You asked for some possible topics and my managers suggested the following:

- *The latest changes to product C*
- *Strategies for introducing customers to the new website*
- *An update on the expansion of the eastern headquarters*

- *Any new trends that you spotted at the Waterloo convention*

Lists are a very efficient way to present information, but they need to have a very specific format. Use bullets when listing a series of items. Use numbers when listing a set of steps that have to be followed in order or to prioritize the list by ranking the information in order.

Rules for Bullet Lists

Lists are a very efficient way to present information in your email, but they need to have a very specific format. Use bullets when listing a series of items. Use numbers when listing a set of steps that have to be followed in order or to prioritize the list by ranking the information in order.

Rules for the Lead In

If the lead-in that precedes the list is a complete sentence, you end it with a colon.

Examples

The following are the four points I'd like you to consider:

Here are the 5 steps you need to follow:

Please answer the following questions:

The material required includes the following:

If the lead-in is not a complete sentence, that means that the material following the lead-in is completing the sentence; therefore, the lead-in has no punctuation after it.

Examples

The four steps require to complete this project are

It's important to remember that

I'd appreciate your input on

Rules for Punctuation

Here are a couple of examples that show how the rest of the list is punctuated.

Example 1

Please complete the following and return them to me by Friday:

- Status Form 1303
- Standard Release 12
- Personnel Questionnaire
- Tax Form C35689

Because the list above follows a complete sentence, there is no end punctuation after the items in the list

Example 2

In order to be ready for the meeting, you will need to

- review the Benson contract,
- bring tax information relating to the Morris partnership, and
- review the Hendley incorporation documents.

Note that in example 2, the list is punctuated as if it were written out as one long sentence with commas after the items in the list. If it were written out as a sentence, it would look like the following:

In order to be ready for the meeting, you will need to review the Benson contract, bring tax information relating to the Mor-

ris partnership, and review the Hendley incorporation documents.

Rules for the contents

All of the items in the list need to follow the same pattern. In Example 2, all of the items in the list are nouns/things. In Example 2, every point begins with a verb/action: review, bring, review.

Here's an example of a list in which the items don't follow the same pattern.

On Friday morning
- Bring your laptop
- Go to meeting room B
- You'll need a 2G memory stick.

In the above example, the first two items begin with verbs (bring, go) and the third item is a sentence starting with the pronoun, you. Since all the items in the list need to match, the third item also needs to start with a verb.

On Monday morning
- bring your laptop,
- go to meeting room B,
- bring an empty 2G memory stick.

Here are two more before and after examples. When you write your lists correctly, it's called parallel construction.

When winter comes, we love to
- ski

- make snowmen
- skate in the park
- making snow angels at Grandma's house.

When winter comes, we love to
- ski,
- make snowmen,
- skate in the park,
- make snow angels at Grandma's house.

Here are some steps you need to complete in order to write a report:
- Brainstorm ideas
- Find research sources
- Draft an outline
- Writing the first draft comes next

Here are some steps you need to complete in order to write a report:
- Brainstorm ideas
- Find research sources
- Draft an outline
- Write the first draft

IN SHORT

- If the lead-in is a complete sentence, it is followed by a colon.
- The items in a list preceded by a colon begin with a capital letter. If they are single words or phrases, they need

no end punctuation. If they are short sentences, each sentence needs a period at the end.

- If the lead-in is not a complete sentence, no punctuation is required.
- The items in a list following an incomplete sentence do not begin with a capital letter and are followed by commas with a period at the end—as if you were writing it out as one long sentence.
- All items in the list need to follow the same format—parallel construction

CHAPTER 3

Tip 3: Easily Confused Words

The words below when used incorrectly are rarely caught by spell checking programs.

Than/then

These two words have very different purposes. *Than* is used to compare: He has more money *than* I have. *Then* is used to indicate time. We went to the bank; *then* we went to the restaurant. One way to remember the difference is that there is an "a" in compare (than/compare) and an "e" in time (then/time).

A lot/Allot

A lot is never one word. *Allot* means to portion out: Because she had *a lot* of candy, she was able to *allot* two candy bars to each of the children.

Their/there/they're

Their is a possessive pronoun. They drove *their* old van to the east coast. *Their* has the words *he* and *I* in it—two people— so it relates to two or more people owning something.

There indicates a place. We left the van over *there*. *There* also has the word *here* in it—another place, just closer.

They're is a contraction for "they are." In contractions, apostrophes usually mean that letters are left out. An exception would be *won't*, but others follow the rule: cannot – *can't*; would not – *wouldn't*. Remembering that will stop you from writing *would'nt* because the apostrophe in the misspelled word isn't replacing anything.

To/too/two

Two is the number 2.

Too means as well. He went to the game, *too*. Generally, "too" is set off from the rest of the sentence with a comma. Sometimes *too* means *extra* and is usually followed by another word that describes the topic: I ate *too* much ice cream. (much describes how much ice cream was eaten.) Yesterday was *too* hot (hot describes the day) She was too tired to go to the party. (tired describes the woman) This is a little easier to remember because there's an **extra** *o* in *too* to go with the extra ice cream, the extra heat, the extra feeling of being tired.

To has one purpose—to introduce something—a noun phrase or a verb. I went *to* the store. We were not required *to* register until Thursday morning.

Who's/Whose

Who's is the contraction of who is. The apostrophe replaces the missing "I" in "is".

Whose is the possessive pronoun. Like all possessive pronouns it shows ownership without using an apostrophe: hers, theirs, its, his, yours.

It's/Its

It's is the contraction for it is. The apostrophe replaces the "i" in "is."

Its is the possessive pronoun.

It's time for the dog to have *its* bath.

Affect/Effect

Affect is the action and is a verb. (A for affect, A for action). After three days of rain, the gloomy weather *affected* our mood. The weather is acting on the people's moods.

Effect is the end product and is a noun. (E for effect. E for end product.) The *effect* of the gloomy weather was to make everyone grumpy. The end product/result of the gloomy weather was everyone's gloomy mood.

Loose/Lose

Loose means that something is not tight. When you *lose* something, it is lost. A good way to remember how to spell the latter is to lose an "o" when you spell lose.

Accept/Except

Accept means receive. Peter *accepted* (received) the award from the president.

Except can be replaced with the word *excluding*. We were all ready to leave *except* (excluding) Bill who was looking for his gloves. Peter can eat anything *except* (excluding) gluten. Since *except* begins with the same three letters as *exclude*, it's easy to remember the difference.

IN SHORT

- Don't rely on a spellchecker to get these words right.
- When in doubt, use a dictionary or use the thesaurus option on your word processing program. In Word, the thesaurus option can be found under the Review tab. Either option will tell you whether you've chosen the correct word.

CHAPTER 4

Tip 4: Paragraphing

Nothing is as discouraging to a reader as a long, solid chunk of writing on the page. If you've written a really long paragraph, chances are that it's not one paragraph. Look for places to break it up into smaller chunks. In Chapter 2, we looked at the option of using bullet lists to break up long paragraphs. Another way to break up a long piece of unbroken text, is to look for places when the topic changes or the when time changes.

Email messages are usually fairly short. It's okay to have one-sentence paragraphs.

Here's an example **before revision**.

Dear Bill, Thanks for asking for my input into the proposed policy changes. I agree that the new policy has many advantages that will be evident to our employees, but I think that one element needs to be explained further. I think it's important that people know the reasons for the new policy, not simply to be handed the new policy and be expected to implement it. Change can be challenging for many, and this policy does represent a significant change. Understanding the reasons for the change helps employees adapt and accept new policies more readily.

This blog post by work-change expert, John Smith, explains what I mean more clearly: http://urlofexpert. I would appreciate the opportunity to speak further with you about the launch of this new policy and strategies to make it more accessible to our employees. Please give me a call today or tomorrow, so that we can set up a time to get together soon.

Best regards,
Heather Wright
Vice-President Administration

Here's the **revised version**:

Dear Bill,

Thanks for asking for my input into the proposed policy changes. I agree that the new policy has many advantages that will be evident to our employees, but I think that one key element needs to be explained further. (**topic change** - new topic starts in next paragraph where the writer adds more details about the key element)

I think it's important that people know the reasons for the new policy, not simply to be handed the new policy and be expected to implement it. Change can be challenging for many, and this policy does represent a significant change. Understanding the reasons for the change helps employees adapt and accept new policies more readily. This blog post by work-change expert, John Smith, explains what I mean more clearly: www.urlofexpert. (**time change** - next paragraph is looking forward to next steps)

I would appreciate the opportunity to speak further with you about the launch of this new policy and strategies to make it more accessible to our employees. Please give me a call today or tomorrow, so that we can set up a time to get together soon.

Best regards,
Heather Wright
Vice-President Administration

IN SHORT

- Look for changes in time or topic to find ways to break long paragraphs into shorter ones.
- In emails, it's okay to have one-sentence paragraphs.

CHAPTER 5

Tip 5: Run-On Sentences
or
What a Comma Can't Do

Run-on sentences are sentences that are really two or three sentences all strung together without proper punctuation.

Example: It's important for us all to attend the meeting on Saturday morning, we have to discuss the gift for the departing president, we also need to talk about the summer barbeque.

The person writing the sentence above knew that there were three different thoughts included in that long sentence and thought that a comma would be fine to divide the thoughts from each other. WRONG. Commas are the busiest of the punctuation marks and can do many things (see the next chapter), but the one thing they cannot do is hold two complete sentences together all by themselves. Here are some correct options for punctuating the above group of sentences.

Use periods to make each sentence correct.

It's important for us all to attend the meeting on Saturday morning. We have to discuss the gift for the departing president. We also need to talk about the summer barbeque.

Use a semi-colon to join two sentences.

Semi-colons are used to connect two complete sentences when the second sentence adds more information to the first.

It's important for us all to attend the meeting on Saturday morning. We have to discuss the gift for the departing president; we also need to talk about the summer barbeque.

Use a comma and one of the FANBOYS.

Commas can join two complete sentences, BUT only when they are partnered with one of the following conjunctions: **f**or, **a**nd, **n**or, **b**ut, **o**r, **y**et, **s**o. **FANBOYS** for short.

*It's important for us all to attend the meeting on Saturday morning. We have to discuss the gift for the departing president, **and** we also need to talk about the summer barbeque.*

Eliminate repeated words and combine the sentences into a shorter sentence.

The new sentence below eliminated the repeated words "we have to" and "we also need to".

It's important for us all to attend the meeting on Saturday morning to discuss the gift for the departing president and talk about the summer barbeque.

IN SHORT

- Commas can't connect two complete sentences.
- Break run-on sentences into separate complete sentences.

- Connect the sentences with a semi-colon.
- Connect the sentences with a comma followed by one of the **FANBOYS.**
- Combine the sentences by eliminating repeated words.

CHAPTER 6

Tip 6: Commas–What They Can Do

Commas are everywhere, but they're not always in the right place. One of the rules for using commas that people often use is to stick one in wherever they take a breath. If that were the case, I would have put a comma in the previous sentence in front of the word *is*. And that would have been wrong. You can never use a comma to separate the subject of a sentence from its verb. The sentence begins with a very long group of words (*One of the rules for using commas that people often use*), but it is also the subject of the sentence, and it can't be separated from the verb *is* with a comma. Uh uh. No. Never.

Here are some places where you should use commas.

Dates
Use commas to separate the date from the year or the month from the year.

September 23, 2016

The comma is not needed when the date is not indicated: September 2016

Place names

In addresses, use commas to separate various parts of the address. There are no commas after the street number.

Toronto, Ontario, Canada or London, England
123 Anywhere Street, Yourtown, Province/State

After introductory words, clauses or phrases.

Groups of words that introduce a sentence are separated from the sentence by a comma.

After several weeks of practice, Jim was ready to enjoy the canoe trip.

Unless we hear from you by January 3, 2016, your account will be frozen.

On Tuesday, we were able to finalize the contract.

I stayed home to study on Monday night. However, my friends went out for pizza and a movie. (These two sentences can be combined into one sentence using a semi-colon: I stayed home to study on Monday night; however, my friends went out for pizza and a movie.)

Before quotations

Use a comma to introduce a quotation.

Hannah said, "I would like to call the meeting to order."

The president remarked, "That was an excellent presentation."

To indicate non-essential information or an interruption

Sometimes we add information in a sentence, but the sentence makes perfect sense without it. In that case, you put commas around the non-essential information. Here are some examples:

I love to try different flavors of ice cream. Jim, as always, chose vanilla.

Every Saturday, though I missed last week, I go to the farmers' market.

If the information is essential to the meaning of the sentence, then it needs no commas.

Athletes who warm up before strenuous activity suffer fewer injuries.

The procedures that are listed in the enclosed document replace section 5 of the contract.

It's important to know which athletes suffer fewer injuries and which procedures replace section 5 in the contract so no commas separate that information from the rest of the sentence.

If the added piece of information or interrupting statement comes after one of the FANBOYS, it doesn't need a comma in front of it.

I was thrilled to receive the award, and as expected, I burst into tears when I thought of my family's support.

Too is a word that is often set apart from the rest of the sentence if it interrupts a statement or appears at the end.

Notice, *too,* that the CEO travelled three times to Vancouver to deal with the problem.

In this sentence commas set apart the word *too* from the rest of the sentence. Use a comma in front of the words *too, also,* and others at the ends of sentences, as well. I like chocolate ice cream, but I like other flavors, *too.*

In a list

When you have three or more adjectives describing a noun, they need to be separated by commas. There is no comma required to separate the final adjective from the word *and* though sometimes it is necessary in order for the sentence to make sense.

It was a dark, stormy and rainy night.

If you wrote that *it was a very dark, stormy and rainy night*, you don't put a comma between *very* and *dark* because the word *very* is an adverb and is never separated from the word it is describing by a comma. Other examples of adverbs include *really, terribly, honestly, literally*, etc. Lots of adverbs end in *ly*, and lots of times, sentences work just fine without them.

The following examples show different lists with the items separated by commas:

Jim ran to the car, tried to open the door, and remembered that he'd forgotten his keys.

When you meet someone new, remember to stand tall, make eye contact, and repeat his or her name right away.

If the items in your list have commas included in them, then you need to use semi-colons to separate the different items in the list.

When preparing for a long trip, it's important to pack all your prescription drugs; a first aid kit that includes bandages, antibacterial ointment, and antiseptic; a list of emergency contacts; and extra batteries and chargers for your electronics.

Here's an example of a list that shows the necessity of using the extra comma in front of *and*.

When Jim accepted his Oscar, *he thanked his parents, Kanye West and Meryl Streep.*

If the sentence above is left the way it is, it reads as if Jim's parents are Kanye West and Meryl Streep. To make it clear that

Jim is thanking all the people individually, the sentence needs to be punctuated like this:

When Jim accepted his Oscar, *he thanked his parents, Kanye West, and Meryl Streep.*

If there is any doubt about making your meaning clear, use the comma before the *and* in the sentence.

Commas and *That*

Commas aren't necessary when you use *that* in a sentence.

Here are some examples:

Jim said that *Survivor* was his favorite TV show.

The shirt that I bought yesterday matched my jacket perfectly.

When Jim was a child, he dreamed that he would be a doctor when he grew up.

IN SHORT

- To learn a lot more about commas check this link:
  https://owl.english.purdue.edu/owl/owlprint/607/
- To practise and check your comma knowledge check this link:
  https://owl.english.purdue.edu/exercises/3/5/15

CHAPTER 7

Tip 7: Fragments

Fragments are bits of sentences that aren't complete but are punctuated as if they were. *Such as this. Such as this* contains no subject and no verb, so it isn't a sentence and can't just sit by itself with a capital letter at the beginning and a period at the end.

See if you can spot the fragments below:

1. Yesterday we went to the shopping mall.
2. We needed to buy groceries plus presents for the twins, Emily and Michael.
3. Because it was their birthday on Sunday.
4. Emily loves anything to do with Dora the Explorer®.
5. Michael likes Lego®.
6. Lots of toy stores with a variety of items on sale.
7. We were happy at the end of the day to have bought everything we needed.
8. Very tired and glad to go home.

Numbers 3, 6, and 8 are fragments. My word processing software only caught number 3 and marked it as a fragment, so don't rely on a green squiggly line to tell you that you've made a mistake.

Number 3 can be fixed by adding it to the sentence above.

We needed to buy groceries plus presents for the twins, Emily and Michael, because it was their birthday on Sunday.

Number 6 needs a bit more work. It needs a subject (we) and a verb (visited). *We visited lots of toy stores with a variety of items on sale.*

Number 8 has the same problem. It needs a subject (we) and a verb (were). *We were very tired and glad to go home.*

When you are proofreading, read each individual sentence slowly. You will be able to hear when something is missing and be able to make the changes you need to correct the error.

IN SHORT

- Fragments are incomplete sentences. They are missing a verb or a subject or both.
- Word processing software won't catch all of these.
- Proofread slowly to catch the sentences that just don't sound right, and add the verb, subject or both to correct the error.

CHAPTER 8

Tip 8: Where to Capitalize

Getting the capital letters in the right place will make your writing look clean and professional. Throwing a capital letter on a random word to make it look important is just wrong.

For example--

Yesterday I heard from Eric about the progress on the Report he is writing with Phil and Alisha. Each of them has taken control of one aspect of the Report and they have asked Lena to be their Editor when the work is finally finished.

Poet Emily Dickinson loved using capital letters for effect, but they don't work so well in every day business correspondence unless they are required. The nouns *report* and *editor* in the above example don't need capital letters. Also, don't go to the other extreme and ignore them altogether. I received a note one year that looked like this:

i'm so glad that you were able to say yes to our invitation. we are very pleased to know we will have you on board for the day. hope everything is well with you. all the best, etc.... This writer went straight from Emily Dickinson to e.e. cummings!

People's names need capital letters, but the nouns capitalized above (report, editor) don't need capital letters.

Unless you are writing in your native language and it capitalizes all nouns or you are channeling Emily, nouns in English only need a capital letter if they are the name of a city, state, province, country, street, school, historic landmark, body of water, etc. Think geography or maps and think capital letters. Days of the week, months of the year, and holidays require capital letters, too.

Directions (north, south, east, west, etc.) don't require capital letters. If a direction is being used to also describe a political entity, then it will require a capital. The North won the Civil War. The names of the seasons don't need capital letters either.

A person's title gets a capital letter when the person's name follows it or when the title refers to a specific person:

- Prime Minister Cameron
- Reverend Jones
- The President addressed the nation.

However, if you are just talking about the job they are doing then you don't need to capitalize the title:

- It must be challenging to be a president of a large company.
- Jim said he always wanted to be the mayor of our town.

For more information on capitalization rules, check the Purdue OWL site.

IN SHORT

- Capitalize days of the week and months of the year.
- Capitalize names of cities, states, provinces, countries, streets, schools, historic landmarks, bodies of water, etc.
- Do not capitalize seasons or directions.

- Capitalize job titles when followed by a person's name or when the job title refers to a specific person.

CHAPTER 9

Tip 9: Who, Whom, Everyone, Everybody, I, Me

Who/Whom and others

Pronouns replace nouns and they do it in two ways. They can be either the subject or the object in a sentence.

Subject Pronouns	Object Pronouns
I	Me
He	Him
She	Her
They	Them
Who	Whom
It/You	It/You

You use the subject form of the pronoun when it is the subject of the sentence. The object form is used after prepositions or verbs. Examples of prepositions are *with, to, in, into, between, without, among, under, above, over, on,* etc.

I went to the store.—*I* is the subject of the sentence.

He went with *me.*—*Me* comes after the preposition *with* and is the object of the phrase *with me.*

If you have two pronouns together or a noun and a pronoun together and you're not sure whether you are using the pronouns correctly, try the sentence with only one of them and see if it makes sense.

Let's say that your sentence is *Jim and me went to the store.* Leave out the word, *Jim,* and say the sentence without it. You recognize right away that *Me went to the store* is wrong. You would say *I went to the store*, so the correct sentence is *Jim and I went to the store.*

Here's another example. *Him and me are going shopping.* You would never say *Him is going shopping* or *Me is going shopping*, so the correct sentence is *He and I are going shopping*.

Remember those prepositions I mentioned? After a preposition, use the object form of the pronoun.

Henry went with Carol and me.

This secret is just between you and me. For this example, I know that you want to say *you and I*, but that would be incorrect. Using the pronoun *I* might sound more formal or proper (and song writers have been using it forever in order to make the rhyme they need) but *between you and me* really is correct. And I'm not the only one who thinks so:
https://owl.english.purdue.edu/owl/resource/595/02/

After *than* and *as*

To make sure that you choose the correct pronoun in sentences using **than** or **as**, always make sure to complete the sentence in your head to help you choose the correct pronoun.

Jim is a better singer than I.

Jim is a better singer than I am.

Linda is as good a runner as I.
Linda is as good a runner as I am.
Mike is as skilled as he.
Mike is as skilled as he is.
Helen is a faster runner than she.
Helen is a faster runner than she is.

Everyone/everybody/each/every etc.

The two tricks for the words in this list and others, such as somebody and everyone, is choosing what form of the verb to use after them and what personal pronouns to use.

Here's an example:

Each of the employees want a raise.

Each is treated as a singular subject, so it needs a singular verb. The correct sentence is *Each* of the employees *wants* a raise. When you are faced with words such as anybody, anyone, each, each one, either, everyone, everybody, neither, nobody, no one, somebody, and someone replace them in your mind with the words *he* or *she*. *She wants a raise.* Another method that will help is to block out the words that are in between the subject and the verb. In the example above, ignore the words *of the employees* and then choose your verb: *Each wants a raise.*

IN SHORT

For more tips on using these tricky words and a quiz, check here: http://www.grammarbook.com/grammar/pronoun.asp

CHAPTER 10

Tip 10: Proofread

Some proofreading tips:

- If possible, put the project away for a few days before you proofread. You're less likely to catch errors if the material is fresh in your brain because you'll be seeing what you're thinking and not what you actually wrote.
- Print out your material. Words look different on the page than they do on a screen. You can spot errors more easily.
- Read your work in reverse order. Start at your last paragraph and work back to the beginning. In fact, reading your work from the bottom up is a great way to catch problems in any project because it makes our brain work a little differently. Our brains are very good at putting words where we expect them to be when they aren't there at all.
- Use your finger to follow under the words as you are reading. This helps you slow down and actually look at the words.

- If you are using anyone's name or title of his or her book or company name or work title, double check that these are absolutely correct. Even the name Smith can be spelled more than one way.
- Let someone else have a look at it. Sometimes a fresh pair of eyes will see things that you don't.

If you want to delve further into the mechanics of grammar and punctuation and do some self-testing, check out the resources at Purdue OWL.

IN SHORT

- Give the project a rest.
- Read in reverse order
- Follow the words with your finger
- Double check names and titles
- Let someone else check your work.

Last Words

There is no magic bullet for success in your career, but you can bet that making a good impression through your communication skills won't hurt and may just set you above the rest.

Good luck with meeting your business goals. One of my goals is to sell more books. If you found this guide of value, please stop by your online bookseller and leave a review. I appreciate your time and your honest comments.

This book is not carved in stone either. If there are other issues about the topic that you think I should address, please drop me a line, and I can always add it to the next edition.

hwrightwrighter@gmail.com

About the Author

Heather Wright is a freelance writer and part-time college instructor teaching business communications. Heather worked for many years in companies, both local and global in scope, and now runs her own freelance writing business. Through these experiences, she has developed her own communications skill set that she now shares in her Better Business Communications series and with her students, in the classroom, as well as in the workplace.